T.V., Sex, and Violence

By R. C. Seely

ISBN-13: 978-1470060350

Property of Mojo Publishing Inc.

Those who do not keep themselves informed of the world forming around them, are condemned to become victims of Serfdom, by those of Authority.

R.C. Seely the Author

Introduction....

    … Before getting to the topics of discussion in this book, I feel that I should tell you a little about myself. To begin with I'm not an attorney, reporter, political analysis, or any profession dealing with politics. For about ten years I was in the retail and sales industry. I've had other jobs as well, I detailed cars, worked as a granite counter top installer, helped put together a store before it's opening, and was an arborist, to name a few. Then a couple of years ago, I went back to a trade school, and got my license in Massage Therapy. My professional training in law was limited to a couple of courses of Criminal Justice, and a course in Paralegal. I do love law, but I don't enjoy college. Otherwise I would have continued in the world of academia and gotten a degree as either an attorney or psychologist. Don't discount what I have to say in this book, though, this is not a book written by a professional in the trade of politics, but it still a valid source of information about the issues. This is politics by a blue collar, everyday man, the ones who made this country. It is what it is. The ones who fought tyranny and injustice, for the opportunity to get a piece of the American Dream, for their families.

    Now before we get to the book itself, I would like to tell you the history behind this piece of literature. This book is dedicated to my Mom, for the influence she has had on my life. The fact is this book wouldn't exist if not for her, because of her over reacting to my Social Experimentation with Rock Music, and Horror Movies, I started this endeavor. It started as, an essay into the study of the Effects of Violence on Culture (Chapter 1), I titled it *T.V., Sex, and Violence,* I put the project on the backburner, because of a lack of reliable information, and high school Geometry. I have since then lost my original notes, which has proven beneficial because of I now have more valid text and improved reasoning skills, to use to my advantage. The other advantage in my favor is an increase in ambition, so I took the original concept of a simple essay, created for semi-self interest reasons, to a book with the imperative of saving the American Way of Life from itself and it's evil twin Pop Culture.

   This book is written in the Revolutionary spirit of our forefathers. This is not a revolution against a physical being though, it's against a destructive school of thought. A cancerous philosophy that was been tolerated far too long, and has proven it wishes not to be satisfied with living side by side in peace. So this my rally cry against the Enemies of Freedom. This is a Pop Culture War.

Chapter 1   Violent Media Creates Violent People...

....I remember this debate as a child, that violence on Television, in Music, and Video Games, encouraging Violence in people. This is something so many religious groups, psychologists, and social activists have clung to. The problem is that evidence is scant at best, dangerous at worst. Lets examine the studies and it's flaws first: Those who conduct such studies already have an opinion on the matter, so subconsciously they taint the results themselves. That's the major flaw with scientific studies altogether, the human flaw is never accounted for in the study, so neutralizing this factor is not even recognized let alone attempted to fix. Even if they don't have a hand in it, the results wind up going their way, simply because that's the point of view they take. Someone like myself, couldn't ethically perform these studies though either, because I have the other perspective. The only way to get to the truth in this is bring in people who don't have a bias one way or the other.

Secondly, as admitted in some of the studies, environment, age, and an individual's biological inklings towards violence, are not always factored in. My theory on that is that those factors are what are actually being what the studies are proving. Violence is a part of the human genome, and that they try to excuse people of their actions this way is, in my opinion, extremely irresponsible. It's like society embracing the idiom, "The Devil made me Do It." The end results of the studies has been that, if parents take responsibility for their how they raise their children, it cancels that out. WOW! Parents being parents, taking responsibility, and taking accountability for their spawn. So could accountability fix *other* problems? Let's try that.

The Bigger point that these Social Pseudo-Scientists haven't considered, is that maybe, just MAYBE, the violence is inherited from Tribal Man. The primitive side that is in all of us, that the Civilized Man tries to kill. Just in some of us it's stronger, than in others. Watch the goings-on during the Election Campaigns, that is Tribal Man, the Survival Instincts kick in, and the worst things that can be said about their opponent is used as a verbal assault, a weapon against his fellow man. It's not rocks and sticks, but the actions are the result of the same part of the Human Animal.

The other consideration in this matter is that this has nothing to do with protecting society, and like everything else, a way of the ever intrusive Government to try to run our lives, instead of letting us live it free. How often has the phrase "For the Greater Good", been tossed around? This isn't new though, during the founding of our nation the federalists, used the expression, for the "General Welfare". If someone does use either of these expressions, they are trying to sell you something. You don't want it though, so just walk away.

Chapter 2 Organized Religion brings People Together...

...In a perfect world, maybe yes, but in this one no. There is a war with Christianity, yes I'll agree on that. The thing is that it's Christendom that struck first, let start with it's exclusionary stance taken up by many of it's members. What am I referring to? How many different forms of this theological movement has claimed to be *the one true faith,* through action, words or deeds. I would say most, if not all. That is the founding roots of it's core, the early days of the Roman and French Reformations were ones of many numerous counts of unimaginable violence against the innocents. The crimes of these *Children of Nature,* nothing more than that they did not follow the crowd, moving to the new Government Religion. They tortured and killed the Pagans and tried to justify it by demonizing them, taking their customs and traditions, and claiming them as their own. It was one of the first cases of Propaganda ever, and it was VERY effective, because it still is raging the world today. I see this a very contagious ailment I call "Idiocy Stupidious Crowdus Variant 1" more commonly known as the Hysterical Mob, and the cure, is Knowledge.

But don't forget the authoritative state of the Church that was rampant in many parts of Europe? Even if you did "Join the Flock", we could still be victims to the numerous human rights violations. If you were a Cardinal or other member of the clergy you do whatever the hell you wanted without facing legal consequences. These representatives of the faith throughout history have taken advantage of this unlimited power and stature, during the Black Plague, the bishops used the situation to fleece the flock. How about Jonestown, remember that? The followers of Reverend Jim Jones, were instructed to drink cool aid with arsenic in it. And they DID IT!! He didn't want to get caught by authorities, so he had to get rid of the evidence (namely all his follows, that numbered in the hundreds) the only one who had it coming was this con artist, he shot himself after his parish died. Dante, what circle of hell did he go to? More recently there have been individuals using this concept called "Rapture", for financial gain. Here's how the con works; believers of Rapture basically get pulled up out harm's way, during the Apocalypse, while everyone else is cut down. But the pet owners don't get to take them along, Oh no, what will we do with Fluffy? What will happen to her? Forget the Johnson's next down, who helped us when our house was on fire, they didn't believe so they're gonna burn. Sorry, guys. Anyway, to protect Fluffy here comes someone who says he can make sure Fluffy's still fine.. For a small fee, like your life savings. People use *some* commonsense. If it sounds like a scam, it probably is. I'm not cynical of Organized Religion without just cause.

The other thing I think is irritating about religion, the Hypocrisy. People who subscribe to organized religion scoff at what others believe, but all of them have their eccentricities, but they think everyone *else*, has the weird believes. The biggest flaws with faith in numbers is people, that's all I'm saying.

Still not convinced? I read about this experiment that was conducted, where these scientists took some samples of snowflakes and altered their shapes using the energies applied to them. One was labeled with the name Adolf Hitler, because the energy applied by the researcher, the snowflake horribly disfigured. Another, was labeled Mother Teresa, and it was near perfect. Yet another in the series, had a prayer by a Buddhist monk performed on it, it too was an almost flawless crystal.

Now take what you want from this but the way I see it, is that having faith, complete is the true power, and it's less important what you believe in. I'm not against organized religion, and I'm not trying to push an ideology on anyone, just the opposite actually. I think too many times society, as on whole alienates people of other faiths, by taking the offensive, instead of trying to understand our fellow man. Instead we should talk to them and find out more about what they believe, and empower them, not condemn them. Besides if Jesus, could forgive the whores and thieves, how can we justify taking these attitudes, and in his name mind you.

Chapter 3 Bush is a Nazi...

...This does have some truth to it, just to be fair. Bush did do a lot of reckless spending and started wars for the oil, both endeavors helped the U.S. Empire and not the Free Republic. He also didn't help make the environment any better for entrepreneurs, or offer already existing enterprises incentives to improve their practices and keep jobs in the country. He also introduced, the essentially, Nationalized version of *No Child Left Behind,* social program. Who could forget the privacy violations in The Patriot Act, giving the government carte blanc in matters of security. All in the name of "National Security."

However, that is not what the context of these slurs were. The whirlwind of infantile name calling and expletives were, you guessed about politics. We saw from the Modern Democratic Party, the worse in the recent past for mudslinging and it's entirely, because he or she, has on R next to his/her name. Or in the case of the other major party, a D. The Republican party, has been showing it's just as capable of this in it's campaign. If they go after Obama with as much force, they could most definitely, take him. But It's not worth it, if you lose your humanity in the process. The ends does not justify the means, and history will condemn you for such heinous transactions. Once the dust clears, whether you agree with him or not, Bush will more then likely be vindicated for his actions. So will any other representative who operates with integrity and fair play. The bigger point is such tactics, can be very damaging to those who employ them, as well as to the party they are associated with. The damage done here can last for years, if not permanently. Is that worth it? Or would it be more satisfying to win, and still preserve your ideals? That is what the founding fathers wanted, no DEMANDED, from those who were to represent this country. I'm sure George Washington, had his moments of temptation, with the idea of being a King, but instead he held true, and was rewarded with something better. A nation unlike any other. I think any candidate, for any position, anywhere, needs to be remember, it's important what do you while your there, but it's also important how you *got* there.

Chapter 4 If you disagree with President Obama you're a Racist...

... If you disagree with Obama you have a brain, and more importantly, know how to use it. I remember first hearing about the man when Hillary was still the front runner of the Neo-Democratic party, and thinking he doesn't stand a chance. He shouldn't have. That was the logical conclusion, he had no platform really, no one had heard of him, and yet, here we are, under the rule of the "Obama-Nation".

So how did it happen, well money for one thing, he meet the right people (this will be discussed later in the book), also opportunity, people were looking for the "Anti-Bush".

The last major factor, and probably the one that was most beneficial for him, the Media. The mass media loves this guy, still does no matter how damaging for the nation he is. To them no can do no wrong, except in reality he has. The claim has been that race has nothing to do with it, yeah right. Race has been the biggest factor in all of this. His supporters have been jubilant, about having a black president. We can claim the race card now, happy day. With every opportunity they have too. My prediction; Obama loses his next election, they pull out the race card one more time. He wins the election, they pull out the race card for the next FOUR YEARS!! That's reason enough for me not to vote for him.

To his credit I do have to commend him on the fact that I don't think that he himself has used the race card, that might be, however, just because he hasn't *had* to. Everyone surrounding him has, giving him a nice little narcissistic bubble. No Mister President, the country doesn't hate you, you're doing a *fine* job. Speaking of jobs, give the man some breathing room you twisted sycophant. Stop kissing his ass, and tell him the truth. He's killing the nation with his policies and needs to be in the unemployment line. Then he will know what it feels like, and maybe, could figure out a way to fix it. When Obama was campaigning, hardball host Chris Mathews, was apparently fawning over the man, acting more like a giddy school girl with a crush, than a hardball political commentator. It got to the point, that even someone like Bill Maher (extremely leftist comedian and political pundit himself) made the comment it seemed, Mathews "wanted to have sex with Obama", with how he gushed about him. Now that's bad.

Chapter 5 Massage Therapy is only for Pain Relief...

     … Massage Therapy has a lot of stigmas attached to it, one that it is only used to eliminate pain. But if you use it regularly as part of your personal health care routine, as well as eating properly, and exercise, your health can greatly improve, and you can cut down on you chances of developing some cancers, heart diseases, and other disorders.

     One of the other stigmas is the association it has had with prostitution. For those of you who fall in that category, here's a way to avoid that. If the word *parlor* follows massage it's, a brothel respectively. It's not like a tattoo shop, where that's perfectly acceptable. The industry is regulated, because of that association. Those days are, for the most part dead. But I don't know that the states really had the problem to begin with, it was mostly in Europe. So you're safe.

     Also just because it's a guy that might be giving you the treatment. don't make assumptions, about his sexual preferences. A lot in the field are straight. Do you jump to that conclusion about your family doctor? Your

Dentist? How about if you have injury, and you need Physical Therapy. Do you think, hmm, I wonder if he is? No, couldn't be. Actually, he or any of the other people mentioned, easily could be, but that's not the point. Making judgments on a person before knowing them, because of what they do for work, is absurd. Women sometimes won't let a male therapist work on her because of the perceived threat of it turning sexual, part of the job is touch, and need I remind you that the sexual misconduct will go both ways. Some women are very amorous, so don't put that just on the guys in this field.

Chapter 6 Country Music is Music...

     … It's not music, not really. It's cats howling, along with scratching on the chalkboard. A little music lesson for you, Country Music evolved from Western Music (Johnny Cash, Merle Haggard, etc.) , which evolved from Irish Drinking Songs, and Irish Folk Music. The bad thing is, unlike it's roots, it doesn't really say anything. I refer to a joke by Larry the Cable Guy, (not Verbatim) " You play a Country Song backwards, your dog comes back, your truck is fixed, and your wife didn't kick you out." I would add didn't have that last shot of Tequila, and wake up naked in your boss' front yard. Both it's roots, used verbal illustrations making comments about the government, and the ailments plaguing society. I can't think of many who have been more beneficial to society than Johnny Cash, or the Irish Drinking Songs, of Flogging Molly. Maybe Metallica with it's questioning the status quo. That's what I want from music, for it to make me think. Let me take that back to include ALL forms of media. Music, Literature, T.V., Computer Media, and Traditional Art. If I can find a deeper meaning (even if the artist didn't intend one) then, my life has been improved. Testing my sense of curiosity, improving myself, learning new things. What could be better? We have this flame of intelligence, that comes from our primeval quest to find the answers to everything. Let it turn into an inferno. All the information, from music and every other form of media, unlocks it all.

Chapter 7 History is Irrelevant...

… History can show us the solutions to current and future problems. The up side being this far in human evolution, is that within the pages of the history books line the answers, to fix pretty much any current issue placed on us. The issues might change, but somewhere we can find another time and situation that holds the key to unlocking that door back to freedom and equality. We just need to start looking. The other plus of having this wealth of knowledge, is that we know what the signs of oppression are. If we learn nothing else from Napoleon and Hitler, it is simply that we need to keep our eyes open for the clues. The change of government can happen in the blink of on eye if we become too complacent, we have been lucky really, we have been given ample time to react.

It doesn't have to be recent history either, or even just our country's own for that matter. Ancient Greece and Empirical Rome, hold many answers, as they have in the past. It's only fitting the culture that influenced our legal and political system, be a reference for us still thousands of years later. Our interactions with others. Our peace keeping measures. Our economic woes. Our civil and human rights, being violated by the dictatorial government. Every single calamity, whether it be by nature or man, the key is the script of our history from cave dwelling tribal clans, to the most advanced civilization, from the planet. History has never been irrelevant, in fact it's getting more and more relevant each and everyday. We have all been too short sighted to notice.

I was reading *The Prince* recently and I noticed certain similarities, between the attributes of the monarchs and our current administration. The same thing with the Roman Empire, and Europe during Napoleon's reign.

In fact if you think about it, the way our legal system operates, utilizes history really. We use past cases to make a ruling on a current one. My last point is simply this; the greatest history lessons of all time are, the ones left by our founders, they are, *the Constitution, the Bill of Rights*, and *the Declaration of Independence*. Without which *the America Experiment* would not have survived.

Chapter 8 Tattoos are strictly for Military or Hell's Angels...

... Tattoos are about self expression. Some people get them to commemorate a place, or time, in their personal history. Some get them because a certain symbol, animal, person, or other object, has significant meaning, or makes a comment about that person. Still others might do it for the same reason our tribal forefathers did it, as a passage of accomplishment in their life. Some just think they're cool. The fact is it doesn't really matter the reason, to anyone, except the one who just got it.

I was watching this show on the travel channel and it had this woman from Scotland, who was setting the record for most piercing. Her face was covered with them, and she's not through yet. I found myself thinking, I don't have a problem with her doing that, depending on her reasoning for it. She was doing it a record, okay, that's cool, but I'm sure she was still wanting them as well. That's what I find meaningless, is when people do things like that, strictly for the shock value.

In the 1940's, we had Freak Shows, traveling carnival attractions, to shock and amaze, the elitist and proper culture of the time. That was the only way one could still be a functionally part of society, back then, and still express yourself in this manner. Some see at as a degeneration of the culture, I see it as an advancement. We are getting more accepting of the cultural diversity, it's not destructive, it's just letting people be who they are.

Chapter 9
Protestors Care
about the Issues...

... Some yes, but not all of them no. Some want the media exposure (dude, I'm on T.V.). Some protestors are paid though, and those are the worst ones my opinion. I read in the *Wall Street Journal* that, one of the protesters, for *Occupy D.C.*, quit his job in Florida to join up with these twits.

I don't know if this is true or not, and if it is it happened quite a few years ago now. I heard a story about a group of animal rights activists who broke into a facility where minks were raised for fur coats. So the group takes all the animals and releases them, however what they did not know, is these minks had been raised there not in the wild. The animals didn't know how the to take care of themselves, and died of starvation.

I do know of a couple of substantiated, cases though. The first involves, an elephant that was supposed abused at a circus by his trainer. Well when shown the footage, the trainer told interviewers, that was not him (and it wasn't), and it wasn't even their facility. What shame you do-gooders. This comes down to the fundamental flaw in the logic of these people, that all animals should be wild and free. The hard truth is that, most animals have a captive life that far exceeds their wild counterparts. But they should be wild they would be much happier. How would you feel if you weren't free? About like now, that's why I writing this book, to protect my right of freedom. Here's the other major flaw in that logic, we are the higher life form, we dictate our situation with analytical thought. We process with our intellect and decide the best action. Animals rely entirely on instinct.

The other was an incident the happened in the state of Utah, when the Tuacahn high school and amphitheatre, was being built, The local Sierra Club, halted the demolition, because the rare Desert Tortoise, was discovered in that area. Here's the interesting part, that tortoise, is not a native species. I sure the owners only caved to avoid the attention, but still, come on people. I'm tired of hearing pseudo-idealists, get away with this. They were legally and ethically wrong. Just because you're passionate about on issue does NOT mean you should get away with breaking the laws to defend it. I've heard the laws for the animal are also as follows, that if one is found in your yard you are legally responsible for it's care. You have to feed it and take care of it. I say we trade some Social Justice, for some TRUE Justice.

Chapter 10 New Year's Resolutions are about Self Improvement...

...New Years resolutions are like taking weight loss supplements, if you're obese. They're not for everyone, a lot of people don't stick to them, and they are not the "Quick Fix" most people want, or expect them to be. I'm very much an advocate for self improvement, don't misunderstand, but it's not something that can realistically done without commitment and hard work. I know some take their resolutions seriously, and to them I say kudos, but I think it's fair to say most don't.

Most just want to keep up the appearance, that they are part of the "norm", desiring to fit in. I think that's why a lot of things like the New Years resolutions have still lingered, it's simply a tradition. It's not a tradition that anyone is particularly, fond of. You don't hear anyone get all excited about making their resolution, like the rest of the traditions of the evening. The fireworks, the kiss at the start of the new year, or starting a new year for that matter. The problem with the New Years resolution isn't that it's not a commendable act, it's a lack of resolve. Most don't give it the thought that it deserves. If they did they would also come up with a game plan to accomplish the task. The other thing that might help is make it a goal you can do with others. If you're doing something like giving up some kind of vice, find someone with that some goal, then the two of you can encourage each other.

Chapter 11 Liberals are Evil...

     ... It depends on which definition you go by. The original meaning is someone who protects Liberty and the advancement of equality. Defends human rights and civil liberties. It's not really meaning the antagonist, for conservative. Being a Libertarian, a liberal in the original meaning, I find insulting, to be considered in the same category as what are referred to as liberal in modern times. In truth if the two philosophies were used in conjunction, that would greatly reduce, if not eliminate many of our problems today.

     By the way the proper term for someone like Obama, would be *Progressive*. Someone who wants everything to be government run, even if the government doesn't know anything about the business.

     When John Locke fathered the movement, I'm sure he never thought it would be used to further the cause of monarchy. Especially, since his intention was the destruction of such oppression. He organized it to protect the people for the intrusion of the corrupt government and church, who at the time were one and the same. He was a pioneer for the age of enlightenment, and was a defender of the constitution. This was the real intention of the movement, not what it has become.

     This is not a new tactic in politics, taking a symbol, or word with a positive association, and altering it to fit your cause. The Nazi's did it with the Swastika, this image original meant unity, a symbol that I'm sure Hitler coveted very much.

George Soros, (he's a leftist billionaire, discussed in more detail later) taking the term *Open Society* and turning it to a society devoid of diversity, which it's anything but. Socialism and Communism, claiming the movements are for the workers, theses movements are to benefit the authorities.

Chapter 12 I'm Right, You're Wrong...

     ... A lot of people say that they aren't wrong about an issue, the fact is majority of what we read is an opinion, presented to us as facts. That's my opinion, but it's one based on a lot of reading, and logical reasoning. So I don't think I'm wrong, when I say that most facts, are actually not anything more than the authors opinion, or interpretation of the issue. I'll admit I could be wrong though, and here's my advice, don't follow blindly what ANYONE says.

     If you want the truth, here's the formula, I've devised for finding it. Find a second opinion; read one book that is favorable about the topic, find and read one that is opposed to it as well. This works with all forms of media as well. I know it's time consuming, but if you want the truth on the subject it's the best way, the truth is almost always somewhere in the middle. Don't have the time or desire to do that? Well, than be cautious, about your information sources. Look for the less traditional ones, or those not in the mainstream. My recommendation is the *Wall Street Journal,* I do a lot of reading, and this is the best source for unbiased opinion.

     Another thing to avoid, is a source who doesn't present any facts to their claims. If all they say is the person who disagrees with them is a moron, but doesn't give a valid argument, as to why, then they are trying to push an agenda on you.

If you're trying to learn more about a specific person's life and accomplishments, try to find their autobiography. It usually winds up being the most telling source of information, because it's where a lot of us will let our guard down, unconsciously let the unadulterated truth come to light.

The all time best piece of advise I can give is, take in the information, and consider it. If it doesn't make sense to you, or something someone has said makes a better point, that's the one to follow. The unfortunate truth is as impartial, as Reporters, Journalists, and Political Pundits are supposed to be, many just aren't, it's part of being human.

Chapter 13 Alternative Medicines are all Scams...

… For some issues, the alternatives are a far better option than traditional medicine. If I have a growth that should be removed, because it might be malignant I'm going to surgeon, don't get me wrong. However if I have a headache (and no other symptoms) I don't take aspirin for it, I have an alternative balm made from essential oils. I use the same stuff, for muscle aches. When I get sick, I drink a detox tea, it's something you can get at Target, Wal-Mart, or in your neighborhood grocery store. The point is don't knock ALL alternative medicines, because of the scams of a few. Tradition medicine has it's scammers as well. Some medical personnel, should no longer have their license, for one. But there are also individuals, who take advantage of people, who should never have gotten it in the first place. Besides, think of how many people died during the early days of western medicine, for those who claimed to be "doctors". Do your research, ask around, and think about it. Remember, too that the way that these medications interact with the body, some can have some serious side effects. Most alternative ones don't, because they are less processed. Look how many of them cause liver damage. Plus the body doesn't usually acclimatize to the alternative, so they are less likely to lessen in potency. The risk of addiction is also less.

The other thing to think about here, is that some alternative medicines have been around for 5000 years or more. Massage Therapy, Acupuncture, and Herbal Supplements, just to name a few. It's funny how New Age, rarely refers to something that is new, it's usually technically a Renaissance.

What I take issue with the most is, what both sides are doing. Demonizing the other. Doctors and hospital representatives, looking down their noses, at Acupuncturists, Chiropractors, and Massage Therapists, and others. Just because it's a different approach, doesn't mean it's not the right one. I've heard some from that list of New Agers, condemn the medical field, as if they still bleed their patients. This attitude is what is wrong, and is unacceptable, from professional healthcare workers on either side of the aisle.

Chapter 14
Americans won't Accept Low Paying Jobs...

... I didn't believe this before, the Recession, I especially don't believe it now. People who don't take lower paying jobs don't take it for a very special reason; the cost of living in that area is so high, that taking that job won't help there situation any.

Sure if you owe ten thousand dollars in student loans you want to keep working no matter what. But realistically you don't want to be in a job that pays minimum wage. It's extremely insulting that the we are in a situation that could have been avoided that professionals, that should be making the amounts they deserve to be making because of the cost and/or technical knowledge needed for their training, need to take jobs like these. Business professionals, taking housekeeping jobs. Healthcare professionals, taking customer service and retail jobs. Educators taking convenient store positions. These are individuals who have paid their dues, and are worse still, having to steal the dues of those entering the work force to make ends meet. Have you tried applying for a job that requires little or no training in this economy? It's hard to even get a response back, because there are extremely over qualified people in the "blue collar jobs" demographic as well now.

Chapter 15 Times Going by Faster...

… This is my own little pet theory based on the literature by Stephen Hawking, and others. Hawkings theorem about time says that, the distance from the earth can alter the speed at which time accelerates. In other words, if your on the ground your clock will read one time, but if you're 20,000 feet up, for example the time will be different, if only by a few minutes. That's due to the magnetism from the planet. This magnetism is due to the revolutionary motion of the molten iron core in the middle of our planet. The inner core in always speeding, but at a lot faster rate than, the earth itself. If it were a solid core, there would be no magnetism, and we couldn't measure time in the way we do (although, that would be the least of our problems).

We have tidal waves on the planet because of the moon, it pulls on our planet, just like the earth pulls on it. So obviously, the moon has an affect on our magnetism, as well as our planet keeping it in place.

Our planet is not keeping it in the exact some place though, the moon is moving away from the earth at a rate of an inch a year. The way this is measured, is by hitting a mirror that was put on the moon, with a laser. Then how long it takes for the beam to return is registered into a computer, which tells us how far the moon is. Still with me?

The fact that the moon is getting farther away leads to the most logical conclusion that, the planet's magnetism is weakening, which would affect the accelerated speed of measurable time. That means while an hour is still sixty minutes, the increments are not as long. So time really is going by faster. The thing is going by the cause of the phenomenon, the moon will at some point no longer by orbiting us, which will effect, our tides. That's not the biggest problem though. If there's no magnetism, we don't have the shield, to protect us from the ultraviolet rays of the sun, or even worst, Solar Flares, or Solar Storms. The good news, this is not this our generation's, or even the third or fourth's problem. The moon is still going to be with is for millions of years, unless something changes.

Chapter 16 Nature and Technology Can't Mix....

     … Most people fall into the category, of either embrace nature, or embrace technology. I respectfully disagree. I feel that this, like most things in life, has the true answer somewhere in the middle. In order to be a truly civilized human being, you have to understand balance. This is the case most of the time too. We are a part of the animal kingdom, so spending some time enjoying nature's beauty can be extremely beneficial, if not at times necessary. But we are being dependant on our intelligence, and our technological advances, no matter how great or small. There was a time when the wheel was a new concept, and our species used spears to hunt with. Both should be revered, and mixed into our lives.

     Here are some suggestions. If you live in the city, not so close to nature, buy a plant. Better yet two or three. Make yourself a little forest in there. Maybe set up a little garden, even just like one of those hanging tomato or strawberry plants. Don't want plants? Okay, how about a pet. I can't think of getting much closer to nature, than having a dog around. Can't have a dog? How about a cat? No, there too, huh? Then fish, a nice fish tank, or a single betta. There are also a wide range of different types of reptiles. Not an animal lover either? Try some kind of water fountain, these come in a variety of prices and sizes, and have very little maintenance. Don't like that idea either? Then go to the park, most large city's have one. Even better, go to a National Park, if you have one nearby. I get close to both by going walking with my Ipod. The point is to be fully functional, at our best, we need to find that balance. Find something that works for you, and enjoy the improvement.

Chapter 17 The War on Drugs is Working...

... Hardly. The War on Drugs, is a Civil Rights nightmare. There is nothing legal, about it. It's one of those laws, established under a moral abjection, instead of Legal or Constitutional Statute.

The reason for starting it was racial, it was instituted in the 1930's, first as a tax, then to counter the Mexican culture. You heard the stereotypes about Hispanics being violent, dangerous, and lazy. Well this is what the administration of the time thought was the cause. Let's ignore the fact that back then (and now really), there was no proof that these substances are anymore additive or dangerous than cigarettes. In fact when the question of legalizing it came up a representative of the American Medical Association, attended the hearing, and he refuted these claims. Saying that, "The American Medical Association knows of no evidence that Marijuana is a dangerous drug." How was his response received? One of the members of congress was reported to have responded, "Doctor, if you can't say anything good about what we are trying to do, why don't you go home?" Typical. It's only valid evidence if *they* say so. They did accept some evidence in that farce, it was by an alleged expert, James Munch, a professor who performed a test in which he injected 300 dogs with the active ingredient in Marijuana, he had the grand total of two dogs die. Very subjective. Let's see him try that experiment now, can you imagine how much trouble he'd get from the Humane Society. To top it all off Munch admitted to trying the drug himself claiming that "after two puffs on a marijuana cigarette, I was turned into a bat." This was at a trial testifying to the "insanity inducing properties" of the drug. So that led to accused murderers of using it as grounds of an insanity plea. So without a constitutional support, in 1970 it was on a list of prohibited substances.

I'm not sure what the justification for continuing it's prohibited status, but I'm guessing to cut back on addiction. That's the selling point anyways, that and it's so harmful. So we going to try things that have been tried before and didn't work. Remember Prohibition, that worked well didn't it? Here's the thing about addiction, whether legal or not, the addicts would still be addicts. There is a big part of the populace that would not try these substances if they were legal, however. How many people have tried Marijuana, just because it was illegal? A lot, probably most actually. So making it legal there goes a HUGE incentive for that percentage of the populace.

There has been numerous reports about legal drugs, like Oxycodone, Vicodin, or Lortabs, that are being sold in the black market as well. It sounds like some would like those taken off the legal market as well. So what are you going to tell all those pain patients? Sorry you're out of luck, because some idiot wants to fry a few brain cells. That's inhumane.

There's an opportunity for a abuse in the system in the fact that an over aggressive police officer can over reach it's jurisdiction and treat a legal painkillers patient as an addict. The optimal solution for all this is to treat it as a medical issue instead of a legal one.

That's not the only problem with it though. The War on Drugs, is also the cause of the violence and corruption, in our southern neighbor, Mexico. Legalization of these substances, and making a American enterprise will not only create private sector jobs, but disrupt the Mexican Cartels, and the corrupt authorities. Something to note, Prohibition was the reason that the Mobsters, like Al Capone, Bonnie and Clyde, and other criminals of the era, gained traction. The government made a law that the people didn't agree with, so in essence, the law was seen by it's citizens as empirical, and the outlaws became the savior.

We have any opportunity to correct a mistake, and generate peace in sector of the world that has not ever truly known it. In the process we stop a process of unconstitutional action that has been allowed to run amuck in our own legal system. We can learn from the mistakes of the past, and improve the future.

Chapter 18 The Internet only has Porn....

       … The internet has a lot I'll agree with you there, but that's not all it has. It also has a lot of information. Pretty much any topic you can think of has between four or five pages, at least, dedicated to it. Wikipedia, one the best invented webpages ever. You tube, also a source of information as well as entertainment. It's an unimaginably effective marketing tool, linking people from across the planet. Myspace, Facebook, Eharmony, Linked In, all sites set up for networking, professional or personal. The World Wide Web, is a part of our world, as much as the fax machine, telephone, and Tim Robbins, for better or worst. Recently the debate over internet censorship was been brought up again, in the unconstitutional SOPA and PIPA bills.

       The arguments in favor of such legislation is so much weaker, that the validations for it's inconceivable. The opportunity for corruption, and eroding effect on the first amendment are STAGGERING. There is no valid justification for such action, and anyone who supports such bills needs to reread the constitution. We can not just go against our nation's policies, especially over moral principle. That would be forcing your views on someone else, which is ethically wrong.

Aside from the questionable ethics and legal conflicts to these such bills. It is completely unnecessary, everything in these modern times has parental locks on them. This has been the solution the whole time. Some say they are not effective enough, okay, then fix them so they are. With the solution already in place why is this still a pressing issue? Control again of course. Control equals power and the more control the establishment can get, for them the better. That is why every time, no matter how you may feel about the content of the internet, it's important to always oppose this.

Chapter 19 Barack Obama is a Good President...

... I guess to some he could be considered as much. That depends on your meaning of "good", first off. Are you meaning "good", as in helped extinguish some of society's woes. Or "good" as in he did some impressive things. In the 1940's *Time Magazine* made Adolf Hitler, their *Man of the Year,* see what I mean about the interpretation of the word "good". Terms like "great", aren't any better, so I say let's not include them in this topic. Let's instead, use the terms, "Beneficial", and make it's meaning in terms of the impact on society. For the other use "Self Indulgent", with obvious reason.

When we change this terminology, it becomes a issue that's a lot easier to discuss, and define.

So let's pose the question redefined; Has Barack Obama been a beneficial President? No, he most certainly has not. He has not done a thing, that is not in self interest of imposing his rule on the constituency. Obamacare, a massive expensive, and unnecessary, measure. It doesn't solve any problems, and will create new ones if not repealed. The Libya invasion, where are you anti-war protestors for that. The bail out, a smoke screen so he can get his hands into American industry. The Tsars, yes it's legal, and yes other presidents have appointed them, it still doesn't make it ethical. Massive government spending, he's spend more than all the other Presidents combined. The deficit was half what it is now. His support of the Occupy Wall Street Movement, he should NOT as a political figure be taking ANY stance, one way or the other on that. Demonizing the business community. This is not the responsibility of the President, and it is a heinous act. Saying that some of businesses act unethical is one thing, but to blame them all for the collapse is just plain, cowardly. It's kind of funny calling him a liberal, in a way, because his concept of Empirical Rule we wants to establish is the greatest Human Rights and Civil Liberties violation to came to this country.

The most disturbing yet, he called himself the best U. S. President there has ever been. Let me explain *why* this statement is dangerous. First, it's suggesting a lack, of a sense of accountability, nothing is his fault that he's done as far as he's concerned. That's a *very* scary implication for *any* representative to take. The other thing about this that I find unnerving, was his list of other great Presidents. He had Woodrow Wilson, Theodore Roosevelt, Abraham Lincoln, Lyndon Johnson, Franklin Roosevelt, and I think Jimmy Carter. Tell you what Obama, give us honest Abe, and you can take the rest of them and move to Europe, okay. I don't even know where to start. Theodore Roosevelt, modeled himself after Andrew Jackson, taken on the monopolistic banks of his era. Problem with that is those days were gone and honest businesses, had replaced them, so the eager beaver "Teedy", was more akin to Don Quixote chasing windmills. Theodore, also helped usher in the Progressive Era, which is when the true Free Market Capitalist system got abandoned, and the Federal Regulations, and the damaging Reforms starts to began.

Wilson, Roosevelt, and Carter, more Reforms, more money wasted. Lyndon Johnson, is actually an interesting choice for Obama, seeing as Johnson was basically a racist. He would change tone of derogatory slurs, according to the company of the time.

The New Deal, The New World Order, "The Obama-Nation" (okay, that's my term for, what Obama would call "Social Justice", but it's still valid), no matter what the name it all smells the same. Oh no, I think I stepped in the Bureaucracy. I got it on my shoe!

Chapter 20 Beautiful People Get Away with Anything...

… If your extremely attractive, and you don't get everything, then it's because you're not trying hard enough. Oh don't take that as a bad thing, I mean that entirely complimentary. The people who would get everything handed to them, are arrogant, self centered, rude, and boring. Superficial individuals like these are rarely into self improvement, so they are not interested with finding out about the more important, deeper things in life. They are satisfied, with mediocrity and want. I know, I was one, although I still as only so satisfied. That's because I knew I wanted more, but I thought that, that world could stave this craving, not at all. It's like being stranded in the ocean, without a canteen. Just salt water, and that won't quench this thirst. If you get all the worldly possessions you can, and you still find yourself feeling restless, you too might be a deep person trapped in a shell of ego.

Chapter 21 Obama Got One Right...

… I'm sure this one has you confused, but he did do one thing that I agree with, he repealed *No Child Left Behind*. Of course, it's only to create some more intrusive education system instead, I'm sure. Actually, he didn't exactly repeal it, anyway, he just let certain states opt out of it. Why just let some of the states opt out? Why not all of them have that option? Or better yet eliminate the program altogether?

If he really wanted to fix the education system, he would get the unions out, and reward the exceptional educators who are being ignored in the system. Yeah, that will happen. I'm sure his solution is to increase union involvement in the schools. Who will hire more progressive educators, because we just don't have enough of those. I remember that vouchers for private schools were also on the table at one point. What happened to that? I used to be against vouchers, but the reading I did has made me think they are not such a bad idea. The competition in the market brought about by the vouchers program, increases the chances of your child getting a best education.

The education system has been taken hostage by the Progressives and they have been feeding children misinformation for over thirty years. That's why keeping the competition in schools, is so important. As is involvement of the parents and community. Teach your children not only what to learn, but *how* to learn. If they learn that lesson, the sky really is the limit for them reaching their full potential.

We as a nation also need to stop competing with the other countries educational standards. Ours is a completely different culture, which when this country was founded was, about Self-Expression, Entrepreneurship, and Industry. Not all the countries we are competing with hold all these values in such high regards. Many don't let the people choose their own profession. Would you really like to live like that? Me thinks not. How about your children? Want them to be basically wards of the state.

The other impediment that I see is the devaluing of the degrees, that has been going on over the years. Ten years ago a Associates degree was of value, not now. Now in some fields, Bachelors and Masters degrees are losing their value. Back in the time of our nation's founders, most professions (including such fields as attorneys) could be established under apprenticeship, and that was the standard that lasted up until the early 1900's at least. President Grover Cleveland got into the field of law this way. As did Lincoln. It was a system that worked. Why change it?

Chapter 22 Famous People Opinions Matter...

... So the theory here is, that because you have money and fame, you are more knowledgeable. Interesting... Not even close to true though. If the celebrities, used their resources to improve their understanding of the issues, then yes. Most however, stick with their vague, and usually false, initial understanding of the issues. The few who do actually have a change of opinion, are influenced not by information and idealism, but by money, power, and propaganda.

Case in point, Bill Maher. Bill Maher, used to both a fair political commentator, and very funny comedian, back when he hosted Politically Incorrect. Now sadly, he's neither. He's gone from an outsider, who was not Politically Correct, to a complete Tool for the Neo-Democratic Party. He takes cheap shots at those who disagree with him, all for the sake of ratings, not for integrity.

The hosts of The View are another example of the embraced idiocy that pop culture deems of significance, on political and social matters. Four very left wing women with chips on their shoulders, and a two bit opinion without the education to back it up.

Next is Oprah Winfrey, people she is a glorified talk show host. Nothing more. Maybe that's what needs to be brought to light. These peoples perspective's are not based on informed, impartial opinion, but the same snippets from CNN or MSNBC.

Chapter 23
George Soros is a Humanitarian...

     ... There's a man, very special man, a very sick and corrupt far left billionaire, who wants to own the world. His name is George Soros. He claims to be a philanthropist, but he has taken a very Machiavellian approach to it, that I didn't even know was possible for a human being to take. I'm not talking about the physics of it, I'm referring to the ethics of it, he basically cripples one company to give to another who agrees with his socialist point of view. This man is a hedge fund manager and has a rather odd, claim to fame. Odd in the fact that he's extremely proud of the odious, and malicious transaction against his fellow man. He is remembered as the man "who broke the bank of England", and here's what he did. He told the community in the financial world to buy up currency against the British Pound, thus devaluing English currency. The travesty is that investors listened to him, so while the British subjects are now in a recession, guess who fattened his pockets... That's right, Mr. Soros. This is a man who does things like this all the time, because he finds pleasure in it, in this real life game of monopoly, only in this game only he gets all the money and the stakes are fatal. He finds joy out of destroying nations. He had played a large factor in the downfall of the Soviet Empire. That's a good thing right? Bringing down the Empire, was the but the way he did it was not. It left many innocent people of Russia, destitute and struggling. Tried to do the same thing recently to our currency, he told inventors to buy gold, up against our own dollar, fortunately, this time they didn't listen. This man sees our country as Empirical, and wants to destroy it. He grew up during Nazi regime (he was Jewish, then), and the Russian invasion of his country, and it made him, a little paranoid. Apparently paranoid, is not something we want this man to feel. Not when we had George W. Bush, the man who started two illegal wars, in office.

This man (Soros) grew up during some of the worst times in history, and while for some that turmoil made them better, increased their humanity, for him it killed every last shred of it. He is completely devoid of any conscience, that moral center that tells us it feels better when we help our fellow man. How can this man claim to be a humanitarian, he doesn't even like humanity. He loathes the human race. He things he is superior.

To quote Francis Bacon:

"The desire of power in excess caused the angels to fall; the desire of knowledge in excess caused man to fall; but in charity there is no excess, neither can angel or man come in danger by it."

He said he would spend his entire fortune to get bush out. He sent in

John Kerry, he couldn't do it. He sent in Hillary Clinton before, but it wasn't her time. So he then sent in a new unknown candidate to fulfill his prophecy, Barack Obama. He has been all to happy to do it as well. I figure, the president has one of the following misconceptions.

Either he feels that the current path of spending his way to an Empire is a financial sound idea, and the system won't collapse, hurting pretty much everyone in the process. Or, he's on the same track as Soros, and wants it to collapse, so they can rebuild into the Utopia. Either prospect is very disheartening. The current president, is either corrupt or naïve.

Chapter 24
Obamacare was the Right Decision...

... Something did, and still needs to be done, this is not the answer. First, it addresses the wrong institution, it's not medical reform that's needed, the problems are with insurance clauses and the legal intrusions in the medical field. Secondly it doesn't fix that problem anyway, it compounds it. Remember HMO's, government intervention into the medical system.

The reason why this bill is hated, by so many, is it's going to be expensive and you don't get anything for the expense for starters. The only reason to vote yes for this would be if it got rid of things such as, denial of coverage for pre-existing conditions, which it doesn't. Why do you need a bill like this? You don't. Those who want insurance can get insurance, don't try to force it on those who can't afford it. That's why this bill was pushed, to tell people what to do. To bully them into a situation. It has nothing to do with what is best for the people. As for the justification for passing it, that's the most flawed logic ever. "We need to pass it to find out what's in it", how moronic! Do you sign a contract without asking what the specific clauses are? I don't know anyone who would do this.

Plain and simple this is healthcare industry being run by business, like a typical business, instead of in a humanitarian way. A little compassion, giving the people the choice. Letting the doctor and their client make the medical decisions, instead of callus bureaucrats, whose only interest is the bottom line. What I'd say is needed is more humanity injected into the system, and letting those in the field decide how to implement it, not having it mandated to them. If given the chance to act on it, charity will flourish with freedom, and people will give of themselves in a very real way.

It's also not morally right for the government to force the people to purchase ANY product. That is the larger dispute in the policy. The level of government involvement in the private sector, by this administration is unheard of and this issue is a prime example of his abuse of power.

Chapter 25 We Need Stricter Gun Laws...

... We need less gun restrictions, and need better enforcement of the few that are actually, beneficial. The less is more, is the best approach for gun laws. For one thing restrictive gun laws are illegal. I'm leaning on an official policy, of no restrictive gun laws. No five day waiting, not even a background check. On all guns as well. From pellet guns, to assault rifles, just as the country's founders intended. Those who want stricter laws, don't want the common man to have the guns for a couple of reasons.

First, they have nothing but contempt, for John Q. Public, and are under the dilution that because they are not of status, they can't be allowed a gun.

Secondly, it's another tool of control.

Lastly, they are afraid of those not of status. Those not of their standing in society may have to create another revolution, they know that and want to make sure we don't have a fighting chance. In perspective I guess Obama didn't entirely lie about "class warfare", he just didn't want the general public to realize the actual perpetrators. It turned out to be the everyday citizens versus the Establishment, just as it has always been.

Chapter 26 Fad Diets work for Everyone...

     ... Fad diets only work for a few, fortunately the ads and products, legally have to say that. Read the fine print, results not typical, change of diet and exercise recommended. What I have to go jogging too, to lose the weight? Forget it, it's not worth it.

     Keep in mind also that fad diets are not individualized per person. It's a mass marketed approach to a basic healthcare situation, but this one needs to be custom made to be truly efficient. Everyone's biology is just a little bit different, so our dietary needs are slightly different as well. We all need a percentage of protein, a percentage of fruits and vegetables, and a percentage of grains. The food pyramid changes from the findings by the experts. Many have said vegetables need to be the highest, some the grains. That's the largest disparity between the studies in general. Some say that beans or nuts are valid protein substitute, for meat and animal dairy products. I disagree, I feel that the way we metabolize food, means we need meat in our diet. We may need less meat in our diets, but it's still an important part of it. Want proof, look at our teeth. We have the teeth of an omnivore, not a herbivore, but in nature even plant eaters are not strictly plant eaters. I saw on National Geographic, a show that included a group hippopotamuses, that took some wildebeest carcasses from the crocodiles. At first the scientists thought they were bothered by their grazer counter-parts being ravaged, until the beasts started gorging on them instead. This is apparently not unique either, some vegetarian species of tortoise will eat meat when it's available. It seems there is no truly vegetarian animal. If done in moderation, meat, alcohol, and caffeine, are fine. The dilemma is most don't exercise restraint, or their muscles. If they did we wouldn't have to hear about all this lunacy.

Chapter 27 Large Government and Small Business Can Co-exist...

        … If you live in a small town, or just happen to live someplace with a lot of local, small businesses, you might have noticed a shift, in the demographic to the negative. Do you know why? Well, that's because here in the "Obama-Nation", no competition to the government jobs, or government approved companies, is allowed.

        Those same regulations on top of the taxes, that the large businesses have to pay, are in place for small business as well. Obama didn't mention that though, did he. As bad as that is for large companies, for small businesses it's fatal. The large businesses have shelter in the market, in the fact that their customer base encompasses the nation in most cases, they have some wiggle room through the hard times. The small businesses have a more generalized, focused customer demographic, however, so when the economy turns sour they are placed on life support. The president has been condemning the use of off shore accounts for tax shelters. Apparently that might have been a most proactive move, because it has saved many companies from it's own government.

The worse of all essentially, all business, big and small that don't give in and take Federal Money (basically buying the company, with, oh yeah, tax dollars. We're funding our own government servitude), will be run out of business. I thought Obama said he was going to protect small business, he lied. In order for his cause to progress, he can't allow any remnant, of the Free Market to survive. If he did then it might spread, then everyone will want to start one, and he wouldn't be able to control everyone. What MADNESS! THE CHAOS!!

There were massive regulations, in the before Obama time as well, but not nearly to this extent. Some are under the impression that it's the government's job to get the economy going again. It's not though, it's the marketplace's, the market will correct itself if left alone.

To demonstrate how out of touch the current administration is with the situation, the president has been claiming, not only the economy is improving, but that he is responsible for the shift. Well I won't argue the latter, he does have a LARGE (about seven trillion dollars and about 12% unemployment worth) stake of culpability in the state of things. Look inside the stores. How many signs do you see advertising 50% or 60% clearances, some I'm sure are up to 70% or possibly higher still. We are in a Buyer's Market, that means the prices are at all time lows. It also is on economic barometer, and it's showing we haven't gotten out from the cold yet. The economy has stalled.

Chapter 28 When we're All Winners, there are No Losers...

      … When did it become a moral wrong thing to be the best? Really? Is this the message to give to the kids? Everyone is the same? So we have abandoned, the lessons of team work, confidence building, and learning to play by the rules. All so little Billy, knows what it feels like to be a winner. So he's getting rewarded for something he didn't earn basically. That sounds like fair play and character enrichment to me.

     Actually what it *really* sounds like is the establishment's, trying to get rid of the next generations will to succeed. Making them a bunch of whiners, because the end result was not in their favor. I'm not going to play with you guys anymore, you cheat. Actually they didn't, but Billy didn't learn that through our failures comes lives lessons. How can this really be justified. What was wrong with letting kids be kids, letting them learn that sometimes life sucks. If they slip and fall, than they try harder next time. Still didn't get it right, try again. Try again, and again, but don't give up. If you don't take anything thing else from this book, take this lesson, and better yet pass it on. To quote the Mythbusters, *Failure is an Option.* Do you the real meaning of what too big to fail is? It means doesn't have a back-up plan. There's an expression for that, that goes, *Who ever doesn't plan to fail, Fails to plan.* Things go wrong in life and the ability to dust ourselves off is an important lesson, don't take that from the children.

As for the bully issue, I think that letting them figure this out on their own is just as important. I don't have children, I do however, have first hand experience. I didn't really get along with the jocks in my school, I wasn't unpopular, they were just that obnoxious at my school. I think most came from well to do families, who let them do whatever they wanted. Anyway, when I had altercations with them I stood my ground. I had a couple of times I had to take a mild beating, but after awhile they learned I wasn't going to take it. Eventually, they backed down, as bullies always do. I'm sure some are thinking, okay smart guy, what about all those school shootings? That's easy that was the media's fault. The incident that started all this is the *Columbine* shootings, and the facts originally reported were not true. The murderers were not the shy outcasts, shunned by everyone. They were quite popular from my understanding, and not the victims in the case. They were just portrayed that way.

Chapter 29 Global Warming (Or Climate Change, Or Whatever the Hell You Want To Call It) is the Fault of Humans...

… I didn't buy into this propaganda growing up, I don't buy into it now. This is all about mankind's desire to be able to make a difference. I have to matter, for better or worse. That's not always a bad thing, but it's an motto that can be extorted. In this case it's an emotion that is being extorted, the emotion of guilt. People will do some strange things out of guilt apparently. But that doesn't make sense, if you give it some thought.   The idea the we could destroy our planet's protective shield is ridiculous. The planet was survived much worse than what we are doing to it, from it's own geological internal processes. You know volcanic eruptions, the gases constantly being released, stuff like that.

The movement in this cause, of the government officials is not because they care about the environment (they might I don't know, but that's not the reason for supporting it), it's because they can hide their plan for their expansionistic agenda. Act like you care, people rally behind you. The fact that they stop at mere words, is far more telling. Remember when Bill Clinton told us it would be ten years before we could get alternative fuels established. If he *really* cared about the cause he would have started the process then, now we would have them.

How about nuclear energy. The chances are next to nothing of anything happening, and every other developed country is using it. Obama picks the only PRACTICAL issue to not be more European. How about Obama's handling of the oil spill. How many days was it before he did anything? Instead of trying to fix the spill, he goes about playing "Blame the Republicans" again. When there's a crisis, the *Presidential* thing to do is to find a solution, fix the problem, and then place blame. I know, bureaucrats don't understand the concept of accountability, but blame comes last.

Some of you reading this are probably thinking, that I'm just cold hearted and don't care about the planet. No, that's not it at all. In fact I'm an advocate for the "Go Green" movement, in general. My opposition is to the GOVERNMENT involvement in the "Green" movement. The President should not be getting involved in it all. Instead he's going against the will of the people and forcing all his precepts of the doctrine, in particularly with the unproven ones on us. The support of the companies like Solyndra, and Beacon Power, were wrong on practical and moral grounds. Moral because it went against the will of the people.

Then he started pushing the hybrids, if he was serious about saving the planet, the fuel is what needs to be changed, not the vehicles. Speaking of hybrids, don't forget about the debacle with the Chevy Volt, the battery that was catching fire. That's some thorough product testing done there.

He has been doing ever option except the one that could work, exploring alternative fuels. Nuclear, I mentioned, can't use coal because it's too dirty. Give me a break! Coal is one of the most cleanest burning fuel sources on the planet. The only options he wants to explore are the ones the cost big bucks, and are not valid replacements, for the fossil fuels. So right now all we have is natural gas, oil, and coal. We can't use oil though, it destroys the ecosystem. Not anymore, it doesn't. With the modern technology, the damage to the environment, is minimal. Obama's involvement in the "green" movement on the other hand, is going to kill the movement, that's what is not being realized.

Besides, this is not the catastrophe we should be concerned about. Asteroids hitting the planet, we don't have a functional system for stopping that. Every hundred thousand years or so, the polar caps reverse, and we lose the magnetic shield completely for a while. Find a solution for that one, then I will be impressed.

Chapter 30
_____ Americans...

     ... I'm sure that will get me called a Racist, but I have to make my opinion out about this known. I'm getting tired of this African-American, Latin- American, Asian- American, whatever country your heritage is from, Politically Correct dribble. No more _____ American.

     My family's origin is Scotland, I don't call myself Scottish-American. People claim it's to be "tolerant" and more "Politically Correct". No it's not. It's so that minorities, can guilt Caucasian- Americans, into supporting all there Affirmative Action initiatives. Those who push for racial equality, don't won't equality, not really. They want Superiority, the same goes for the gay and, the modern Feminist movements. The term Tolerance, means for them, nothing less than Acceptance. Total and Complete submission to their agenda. Just to get something straight here, I'm not racist, sexist, homophobic, or any other, -ist there is. I have always had associations with people of different races, I have a good friend who's a lesbian, and I'm all for women's rights. I just want to be left alone. Is that too much to ask? I won't be bullied, into accepting a point of view I disagree with, and neither should you.

Another, thing, all this whole _____- American movement does in divide the country, and keep the bigotry alive.

In order for Mahatma Gandhi to get a peaceful India from the tyrannical grip of the British Empire, he was forced to abdicate to the isolationist portion of his country and make a enormous sacrifice. Segregate the Muslims from the rest of India. Today that isolationist state is Pakistan. Why is that a erroneous blunder? Because it compounds the rampant aggression and, breeds more violence and dissention in an already volatile set of circumstances. If the factions are forced to co-habitat, they will eventually find some common ground and a comprise of peace can be achieved, for the region.

In extreme cases the only solution to this process, is to let it play out to the point of war. It's sometimes the only route of resolution. Instead the course of indulging this segregation, and the nation was permanently divided without hope of reconciliation. That was more than likely the Mahatmas' greatest regret. He left his compromised India with a feeling of failure in his heart.

This is what is happening in our country. The lesson here is quite apparent. Caving in on this on is diluting the melting pot, and dividing us as a people and separating the country not fusing it. People of other cultures can keep their customs, but if you are not from here than you sure be altering your behavior and assimilating, not those already here doing so. This is all a big ploy so favoritism can be shown to the minorities and special interests representatives, so they will vote for Obama, that's all.

Chapter 31 Fox News is Fair and Balanced....

... Here's a little challenge for you; Watch Fox News one day, and then watch CNN, or CSPAN, tell me don't see the difference. Watch MSNBC then you will. I hate MSNBC. They never make their point, but can't admit they might be wrong. Not even a slight chance, you don't have all the facts? Alright, Chris Mathews and Rachel Maddows, but you backed Obama, so you were wrong at least once. The fact is Fox News is Fair and Balanced, because it was formatted to be outside the mainstream organization. Think about it. It's the only news network that has fairly equal percentage, of Republican, Democrats, and Independents, as commentators. Where as the others have, well, none.

When the other networks have brought them on, they have forced them out because of company politics. If you are not conforming to our ideals your out. An independent thought, what's that? Here's some names you might know. Lou Dobbs (formerly CNN), Juan Williams (also formerly CNN), John Stossel (used to host 20/20 on abc, I don't actually know why he left), Glenn Beck (formerly CNN, now no longer with Fox though, but he still counts). Most left because they voiced contrary opinions, and we can't have that. When did journalists lose their integrity? So many have sold out for ratings. I wonder how many actually do subscribe, to the agenda being placed on them. People will sell their soul for their career.

Chapter 32
Astrology is not a
Valid Science...

        ... Astrology, like all sciences is not perfect, but that doesn't make it invalid. The influence of Astrology is actually fairly ingrained in society. Navigators will still use it when necessary. Many cultures used it to develop their calendars. It had influence on alchemy, astronomy, meteorology, and even medicine. It was in combination with other occult tools, is how Nostradamus, made his predictions. It's how all ancient tribes set up their civilizations, which in turn lead to the civilizations of today. I do believe in the authenticity of the possible applications of it. It can give assistance in our everyday lives, if we are open to what it has to say. My observations have been it's very accurate on predicting the personality of the individual born that particular date. If you can find the exact time and place, it came be even more accurate. More importantly I find the attitude about this more alarming. When did the scientific community get to so cynical. They used to battle the skeptics, and now they are the skeptics. That has become the attitude of the mainstream at least.

Chapter 33
12/ 21/2012....

　　　… Before I go into the addressing this topic, I'm curious, how many of the populace know the significance of this date? It is the infamous day, when the Mayan Calendar ends. The Doomsday Clock, as it's called runs out. Here's the thing. Like a lot of other terminology being addressed in the book, this is another inappropriately, termed topic. This phenomenon is being circulated by the worse kind of pop culture, shock culture. Other examples are the talk shows (Montell, Jerry Springer, and those ones) and the tabloids.

　　If you were to look up subject, by those have actually STUDIED it, you would find out how benign this occurrence is. The ending of the calendar is a time "big change", it might not even be anything bad. That doesn't sell though. Look at the profits made with the millennium scare. The Y2K fiasco sold out like, a AC/DC concert, and the pop culture media made massive profits. Don't forget the other entertainment fields. They had a television series called *Millennium*, dealing with the paranormal. It was by the same creator of the *X Files*, and they had a cross over episode for Y2K. Also there was a movie with an association to the millennium, *Entrapment*, it starred Catherine Zeta Jones and Sean Connery. It was a action movie about a big heist. There was a movie called *2012*, about the 2012 event.

This is not the first time the entertainment industry has been capitalizing on disasters. Remember *Jaws*. Or *Earthquake*. *The Towering Inferno, Armageddon, Deep Impact,* just to name a few more. The major difference here, is that the millennium caused major social distress, robberies, and even mass suicides. There has to be more discretion, taken by those reporters, of fictionalized such issues.

Chapter 34 Primitive Cultures are More Simplistic Cultures...

… In some ways they were far more advanced, than modern society. Especially, in their association with nature and the family bonds. I'll bet they had all the same gifts that our friends in the animal kingdom have. Like when a dog or cat, acts differently to warn of an upcoming storm. They lived in tribes, and protected that tribe. It was a very efficient system for their society. They looked out for each in their tribe, and their culture advanced. The only real negative effect was that they had to massacre other tribes to accomplish this. So from a nation wide culture with such a large diversity, it could in no real way be considered civilized.

Don't forget that many early cultures had such amenities, as spas, and indoor plumbing, as well. So human rights aside, there was some headway towards civilization. At times it's not always obvious, that that cultural evolution has occurred.

Chapter 35
Switching to the Euro was Meant to Bring Countries Together...

   ... The Euro was made to unite, Europe, yes but not in a way to bring them together, but to dissolve, all diversity. Why? I'm not entirely sure, why they thought this a good idea. I know it was an impractical idea, though, as is now being shown. It's intention was to maximize economic efficiency, in the region. The cause of the international disaster that came about, was due to the lack of monetary disciple in some of the countries in the region. Greece, Ireland, Portugal, to name some of the major offenders. It has been a blessing for the countries in debt really, because it makes it harder, for the other countries to just abandon them to figure it out. It's kind of been a raw deal, for, France, Spain, and England, though. They were financially responsible, and didn't deserve it. Now no one can run somewhere else for help, because everyone has their hands tied to this. This is the dark side of Globalization. The act of essentially intertwining nations, with connections, economic, political, social, etc. The consequence of this is that we all go down together in this model.

Chapter 36 Things Were Better under the Gold Standard...

    … If we had never gotten off the Gold Standard, then the country would have been able to avoid the current currency fiasco we are in right now. Here's a lesson in economics, paper money is basically worthless. That is why Progressive lawmakers love it. So easy to manipulate. If our currency was still backed by gold or some other precious metal, then this can't occur.

  Some blame the gold standard for the length of the duration, of the Great Depression, that's an absurd assumption, done by those in favor of expansionist policies. Ben Bernanke, being one of them. Yes, I want his opinion on common sense fiscal policy. What made the Depression longer, was that the other countries panicked, and transferred their gold reserved out of the U.S. causing the dollar to devalue. The loss of faith by the other countries expanded the depression, the gold standard protected as more than hurt us. The value of Gold was lessened and we got out of the Depression. We have been victims of other countries is the reasons the Gold Standard in our country didn't work, not because it was a bad thing.

That's why Richard Nixon, did the worse fiscal decision possible, he took us off of Gold. The French president reduced his monetary reserves trading them for U.S. Gold reducing the dollars value. Than the fact we were in the Vietnam War, and it's mounting costs, plus plaguing payment deficits, he made the monumental and fiscally fatal choice. Ever since then our paper money is our currency, a currency with nothing behind it. An I.O.U. basically.

Chapter 37 Making Prostitution Illegal was the Right Thing to Do...

     ... This is another legal statue established, because of a moral objection, not a constitutional judgment call. People find it abhorrent, to pay for sex, but some think perfectly acceptable. The thing is no matter what your moral stance is on this issue, it's not right, to project it on others. That is what I have contention with.

     The bigger reason I opposed having this illegal, is because it has created a victim society. With it being illegal, these women can't really go to the authorities, when being victimized. Now the rapists and serial killers have victims to hone their skills on. Their have been a lot of the ilk of different cultures that have taken advantage of the situation. At least our culture, killing them is illegal. In ancient Rome, for example you could legally, kill them. In other countries it's a regulated profession, that makes large amounts. The estimated revenue world wide is in the billions. It would end poverty is another argument, that could have some validity to it. The ladies would be contributing to society, in financial way.

     Aside form the ambiguous and vague legality of it and the culture of victimization produced by it, there's another reason to revisit the status of this statute.

There was a incident when Mitt Romney was head of Bain Capitol, when an association of his was facing a family crisis. His friend's daughter was at a party, was drugged, and had gone missing. Romney took a flight to where the incident occurred, and had his staff assist with the investigation.

Anyways during the investigation drug addictions, homeless, and prostitutes were questioned, about their knowledge of the events. The woman was found and things worked out...That time. This is not always the case, because these women don't have much encouragement to cooperate with authority figures. As well as being the victims with the culture, we'll have created a incentive for them to aid in restraining violent criminal acts against law biding citizens.

We already have a legal system that encourages their aid to a degree, but there's also a counter-culture that damages this tenuous relationship. There is the Vice Squad, who makes their life hell, and yet other forms of law enforcement depend on them for their interventionist status, of street interactions.

In the illegal immigration tie we would hinder the human slave trafficking in our nation as well. Because with this (and the cessation of the drug war), as with the before mentioned conclusion with the continue status here the culture of victimization for the immigrants, would go unscathed. It might even damper the illegal immigration predicament to a degree at any case. So many of these cases end up like this, fix one challenge, fix at least a couple more.

Chapter 38
Construction and Infrastructure Projects Build Jobs Better than the Private Sector...

… Government influence in the job market, always ends up going the same way, more waste, corruption, and inefficiency. From the times of ancient Greece, the Rome Empire, to now the "Obama-Nation", it's the same damn thing, with the same results.

When government gets involved then companies barter in favors. It's like in the Mob. You scratch my back I'll scratch yours. I'll make sure you get elected, but you owe me. He just bought himself a politician. In this case the politician is the mobster, and he just bought a company. It's now the unions who own the politicians. In a lot of ways the mob doing this is preferred, they are doing illegal activities and there's little dispute. With the unions doing the same thing for some reason, it's considered legally valid. It's all in the name of Progress. The model the Progressives are using here comes from the economic theory by John Maynard Keynes. Essentially, according to the theory, it's the government's responsibility, to fix the economy during turmoil in the marketplace. No it isn't. If the President had stayed out of the marketplace and let those in it fend for themselves, it would have been fixed by now. But no, he had to get involved and slow things down.

Chapter 39
Teaching
Abstinence is Best...

… Teaching just abstinence is ridiculous. Let us put aside the moral objections for a minute, and consider the ramifications of this. You're basically putting all you hope on your child not having sex. Next to food, going to the bathroom, and sleep, the last basic need in most multi-celled organisms, is reproduction. Did you see how idealism can blind people? I'm an idealist myself, but I prefer to get the facts first. If your children are not taught, about safe sex and they are in the portion of the populace who are going to still do it, then they will have unsafe sex. Congratulations, you're child just became a statistic. I'm sure you're so proud. If you want your children to wait then tell them that. Is that so hard? The fact is in the end, they will decide to do whatever they feel is the best choice for them no matter what. Doesn't it make more sense, to let them know the safe way? This is not condoning the behavior, it's protecting your child. You know, your main duty as a parent. By this involvement you are showing accountability, as well, and maybe the child will pick that lesson up.

Here's the major point of contention for me, abstinence is supposed to a conscious choice, but under this concept how can it be. The kids are getting pressure by the school, their parents, their church, and from other students. This is still peer pressure, just because it's trying to help them make a decision that could avoid some retribution, doesn't mean it's not. Someone is trying to make one of the biggest decision, for the child instead of giving the child the information, so they can decide for themselves. It may or might not be right, the actions are wrong, and the how just the cause is doesn't validate it.

Chapter 40 The Occupy Wall Street Group are Right...

… Let's start with violations to polite and civil society. The occupy wall street group, has been reported to have defecated in the streets, building tent cities, vandalizing property, and in extreme cases, rape and assault. I will give the Occupy Wall Street group credit, when it first started, they were doing things the proper way. Then an anarchist branch came through, that's when the group really got a bad rap.

I'm not against protesting. I don't do it personally, but if it's done according to the legal statutes of the city, and it remains non-violent, then go ahead. What I'm really against with the occupiers, is that they are not informed. It's just another protest group who didn't do their homework. The group says they are against inequality in the marketplace and class warfare. They don't know what class warfare even is, it's not about the rich versus the poor. It's about human rights and civil liberties violations. There were atrocious working conditions during the industrial revolution, that meant it was very dangerous to go in and some of the employers were capitalizing on that. It wasn't about the financial divide, and how it is they can't understand that the wealthy make the jobs is beyond me. I'm below the poverty line, so this is by someone in the same financial bracket (or even lower, than the protestors) , but I want those with money who have earned it ethically to keep it.

Let me explain how redistribution of wealth really works. The government takes the money from the wealthy, and puts in a slush fund, from there, first dibs goes to the unions, then the special interest groups, then the companies that the government bought (this is in the form of bailout money), that the have to take to keep their license, and then it gets to the public. I mean you didn't really think that they cared about you?

Chapter 41 Being Patriotic is Morally Wrong...

… If your patriotic then for some reason, you're in the wrong. The reasons I read are because patriotism is an emotional state instead of a logical one. Fair enough, maybe it is all just an emotional one. Maybe, in some instances it is used to control people, or impose their values on others. That goes both ways though. The argument here is that if we're patriotic than we might try to put ourselves up on a pedestal, and try to impose our will on others. Try to change their culture into ours. A lot of the people of the other nations, first off are not against the American way of life, just our political leaders interference in their affairs. Who could blame them really?

The other flaw in this logic is saying that this model of political thought can't be manipulated. The Non-Patriotism machine is just as easy to rig, as those of us who put faith in the country. The fault with both schools of thought, lies on the action's of the individual. I'll tell you though, people who are Patriotic, are more willing to individualize, because they see the value of freedom. The unpatriotic want to change this country for the worse. They are sure to lose this cause, those defending their nation, are more likely to die for that, than those defending just a principle.

I'm sure some think I'm trying to reach the unpatriotic, I'm not. Frankly I don't care about them, for me they are not worth it. I don't think they deserve what they are given by living in this awesome country of ours. It has it's problems, yes, but it's still an amazing concept from an era long ago. I think these are the kind of people who are looking for perfection, and when they don't find it, feel the need to ridicule the world or at least their part. I think we should send them to a third world country, give them some humility, that's all. Just like I think those who want socialism to come here, should spend some time in a socialist country. Try it before you make your final judgment. At the very least talk to someone who has.

Some of them feel patriotism is a learned trait, maybe, I grew up in a very patriotic home, if I didn't I might not be writing this book (at least not from this perspective anyhow), I might have grown up not caring about anything. I might have become one of these snide hipster Progressives, thinking that this country would be so much better, if the government gave everyone everything, instead of making us earn it. If your in a government that gives you everything, that's basically it, you can't make more than that. I'm glad that I live where I have the opportunity to pursue happiness and that's why I'm patriotic.

Chapter 42 Welfare is Working...

… Not exactly.. The Welfare system, and unemployment for that matter, reward those who don't want work as well as those who can't work. This violation is basically glossed over by authorities, if not in some cases encouraged. We need to fix this and make sure it is no longer allowed.

Also both systems, in modern times more seem to punish those who want to work. At one point you had to prove you were looking for employment, to get assistance. Is that still what's in place? A lot of people have just given up looking. Many of them want a job, not a handout. That's what the country is giving them though, and many more will be joining them if we don't fix this system of dependence soon. I hate to suggest something from Newt Gingrich (he's a Progressive, yes they come in Republican as well), but he did have a good idea for the unemployment conundrum. Instead of just giving them their checks, get them enrolled a training program, so they can develop a trade. That way when the economy does gain momentum, they have another set up skills to use.

We also have the same flaws in the foreign aid department, only with some more added dilemmas. First how can we possibly ethically, let alone financial, justify administering aid to other countries when ours borrows, from China? This isn't chump change we are borrowing either. An economic lesson for you, the way we got to fifteen trillion in national debt, was not just Obama. It wasn't just either of the Bushes. Or Reagan, Carter, Nixon, or Johnson. This started at least with Theodore Roosevelt, if not even sooner. That's the *1800's* people. That's how ingrained this pattern of spending is. Did you know that the unused money borrowed is what a surplus is? How idiotic! We need to make the hard choice before we reach the point of no return. Lessen government power, and stop the entitlements systems.

The pathway to this is to stop government spending. Then bring the troops home, and place them at the border. Than the money that would have been spent on the unrealistic war effort, is funneled back into the economy. See two problems solving, that's multitasking.

Chapter 43 Capital Punishment doesn't Deter Crime...

… Maybe not, but that's one less person to do that crime. Okay, here's how the system works; someone commits a crime they go through the legal system and get a ruling, if it's heinous enough they get the death penalty. Either way if it's a violent crime the victims families get to confront them, and with the ruling they get closure. Some claim that Capitol Punishment isn't valid and doesn't work. It gets one more dangerous individual out of the populace, that's good enough for me.

If anything I think we need to extend the death penalty to offenders of violence to children, and rapists. Make the standard of guilt higher maybe, but if found guilty, then get them out of society. It is a tragedy when an innocent person gets put on death row, I'm not saying it's not. That's on the defense. If a guilty person gets off, it's on the prosecutor. The survivors of the death row inmate, also get my sympathies as well. It might not be an entirely Libertarian point of view, but that's how I see it. Violent offenders need to be separated, and the other inmates, should be on work detail. We get some labor out of them, they get out their cells in a safe way to the public, and the dangerous don't get to violate the law binding citizens.

Chapter 44 The Moon Landing Didn't Happen...

… Seriously? How many people really think this? Of course it wasn't faked. This is one of the most absurd conspiracy theories ever. Remember in the chapter of this book about *Time Going Faster*, I mentioned that on the moon there is a laser that we use to measure the rate the Moon drifts away from the Earth. If we hadn't been up their how did that get up there then, huh? I'm sure the conspiracy theorists will come up with some ludicrous answer, but how about instead you let it go. I'll admit there are plenty of reasons not to trust our governmental officials, this is not one of them. This was tested on the show *Mythbusters*, and they kind of proved the point that it happened. The conditions can be faked, but they would not have been KNOWN about those conditions if not for going up there. Besides with John Kennedy's resolve to beat the Russians, he would have made sure that getting their first was the real outcome of the country.

Here's another fact that should be included in the conspiracy, the moon landing conspiracy started gaining traction in the post Watergate era and the general opinion about the government was at an ultimate low, than it would be only be logical it was given more credence.

Another reason this opinion should not be considered valuable is that one of the countries with the highest numbers subscribing to this consensus, is the Russians. Our competitors in the Cold War, the reason why we went up to begin with, means by logical conclusion such a theory should be discarded like old chewing gum.

Conspiracies are created as a diversion, to get people to watch one thing going on, and divert them from something else. My advise, pay more attention to what the other hand is doing.

Chapter 45 Unions Help the Workers...

… The labor unions have helped those they represent on occasion, but for the most part they help make themselves rich, at the expense of others. That is why the private sector doesn't like them. They cause problems for employers, just so it looks like they are doing something for the members dues. Unions are about as corrupt an organization as you can find however. They encourage violent action, destruction of property, and mass riots. I used to think that was only true of modern unions but the ones of the past were even more notorious for their crimes against humanity. The only issues that these organizations have any right to get involved in, are safety and human rights violations. Thanks to the fact that most of those are for the most part a thing of the past, in order to have something to do, they go and cause trouble for the CEOs. I'm not claiming that every business is honest, I know that's not true. But these are people butting in who haven't served in the business world I'm sure. Maybe the heads of bureaucratic special interest groups, but not as the head a fortune five hundred company, no. I'm not going to beat around the bush, I think we need to start the process of defunding the power houses. What will we do as an alternative? Simple, let the private sector fill that economic niche. We now have seen what doesn't work, as an organization to protect the safety and wellbeing of our fine work force. Now let those who know the ins and outs of the business world, take over and replace them.

The major problem with unions, is that they have too much money and power. They have been putting their money towards the Neo-Democratic party, for along time and they have been stacking the dice for people like Obama. The unions are so beyond corrupt they also have ties to organized crime. That's not exactly a big secret though. That's why Jimmy Hoffa got killed, because he refused to play the game. There is a positive shift in all this though. Union membership are at an all time low. The numbers report the private sector at about 12% and the public sector at about 37%. It has also reported that it hasn't been this low since the Great Depression. So keep a look out for some pro-union advertisements. Remember this, the unions are trying to take your job to give to a union man. If you want our nation to improve, help fix the problem not become part of it.

Chapter 46 Hippies are Anti-Government...

   … The movement claimed to be, and I think some of the crowd thought it was too. All it wound up being about unfortunately, was making a larger government. Somewhere along the lines the flower power generation changed from trying to fix the country's problems, to making them much larger, to creating substantially more devastating new ones. The goals idealized in *Woodstock*, were about Peace, Love, and Happiness. Trying to make the world a better place, when did they get off track. Truth is I'm not sure they ever really were. This was really all about the power and money that this revolution could gain, and distribute. This is one of the oldest tricks, in the arsenal of these radicals.

   Saying one thing and changing the meaning, the only difference here is instead of a word being changed this time it's the whole message. Seeing as I've already addressed this I'm not going to again, but rather take the opportunity to give you something to consider. Let's try adopting the original message. Peace, Love, and Happiness. When those that hurt us do so, turn away. Don't engage them, but stand tall against them. Show them that they can't change you from the right direction. Show them they have no power over you. Then you will hold all the power, because you took a step in the right direction yourself. The direction of Peace, Truth, and Prosperity. One person might not change the world, but they can just maybe change their part of it.

Chapter 47 NPR Reflex's Public Opinion....

     … Maybe, but not of the majority of this country, though. When I was in Las Vegas, to take my examine for my occupation license, I stayed at the *Luxor* hotel. I received a complimentary copy of the *Las Vegas Review* during my duration there. While I was reading it, it dawned on how the paper was trying to sell the Democratic party, by saying they embraced the more conservative (or Libertarian) ideals. They were basically trying to recruit potential democrat voters, by enticing them with tax cuts.

     This got me thinking, is their some potential for some real reforms to our failing system? Could this all be because Pop Culture is misleading, the people to the Obama Monarchy? I'm not saying that the last administration, didn't have destructive policies, but he didn't lead the country down this path of self demise. This all comes down to the same thing, knowledge. Don't just accept what is told as fact, find out for yourself if it is.

     The fact is most of the Media wants the Obama agenda to succeed, because they gain to prosper from it. They have been protecting him, and will continue to do so. NPR is on that list. They embrace his doctrine, and, through PBS, teach it to your children. The American people are being brainwashed into this with false truths, and flat out lies. I remember it when I was growing up. There was a cartoon on called *Captain Planet*, it was the most ridiculous piece of hype I ever saw. Now it's been getting worse and worse. It's in the education system itself. Public television is most definitely a massive propaganda machine. It doesn't reflex public opinion, it manipulates it.

To quote a line from, *Oscar Wilde's, The Picture of Dorian Gray*:

"Because to influence a person is to give him one's own soul. He does not think his natural thoughts, or burn with his natural passions. His virtues are not real to him. His sins, are borrowed. He becomes an echo of some one else's music, an actor in part that has not been written for him. The aim of self is self-development. To realize one's nature perfectly- that is what each of us is here for. People are afraid of themselves, nowadays. They have forgotten the highest of duties, the duty that one owes to one's self. Of course they are charitable. They feed the hungry, and clothe the beggar. But their own soul's starve, and are naked. Courage has gone out of our race. Perhaps we never really had it."

That cynicism is very pertinent, then as well as now. Which is why questioning our establishments are the only way to secure our freedom.

Chapter 48 The Two Party System is the Most Unbiased Option...

… The two party system has not worked very efficiently and isn't unbiased by any means. It's about as biased as it comes. It is not conductive to a debate, because everyone is siding with their party and not willing to meet halfway. Some issues being unwavering, is imperative, true but on many a little give and take can be just as crucial. Figuring out a middle ground is the mark of a great diplomat, and that is definitely a plus for the nation. In general though, leveling out the playing field and introducing the other parties into the debates, would be the most proactive step towards meaningful reform. Remind the people that they have more options, than just the two. Then we could really get things fixed. Both parties are loaded with corruption. They've been in power too long, that leads to an addiction to power. Both have long since sold out, either through dealings with the lobbyists, special interest groups, or in some cases each other. When they are not making the deals with the other party then they are making back door ones, from the public.

The other side effect of this arrangement, is the protective media bubble that forms around those of the party establishment. A lot have seen it around the current President, but are blind to it surrounding the contender representing the Republican establishment. Newt Gingrich, is not the conservative agent he represents himself as. Nor was the last contender for his party, John McCain. Both are advocates for intrusive, large government and spending on social programs. I'm not against spending being done on such projects, but I know many feel such policies are subversive, and forcing *them* to financially support such agendas is morally apprehensible. Both parties are very guilty of this and the practice should be halted. The only things the government should be funding, is the protection of it's people, and the judicial system.

I also have to say that I find it rather disturbing that not one democrat has the backbone (or the ethics, whichever it is), to stand up against Obama. It doesn't really matter if he has a chance or not, but doing so would be a strong showing of principle, which is very much needed right now.

To get to this we have to take one more step though. Stop diminishing the opposing party for their different point of view. That's not saying don't call them out on impropriety in conduct. I'm saying consider the reality of the situation we are in and consider their side. No more ignoring liberals quest for humanity, or for the other side the need for fiscal efficiency and at times restraint. No more absolutes from either party. These don't help get things accomplished.

It's also not conducive to do cheap shots at the other party, or each other. Like the one that Newt Gingrich did at Romney, with his misquoted statement that he's, "not concerned about the poor." Come on Newt, get the gloves up.

When the founders set up the country, it was not the Republican Party versus the Democratic Party. It was the Federalists versus the Republican/Democratic Party. At one point the ideals of Anti-Imperialism were revered by both of the major parties and now are not revered by either. At some point in our future we will need to abandon the two party system, or this cycle will never end.

Chapter 49 Michael Moore is a Documentary Filmmaker...

… Michael Moore is the maker of The America Snuff film. Every movie he makes since becoming a "documentary filmmaker", is made to kill the nation, and warp the culture to his socialist doctrine.

He's doesn't film a true documentary anyway, because what his documentaries are, are not the truth. The movie *Fahrenhype 911*, made to counter his film *Fahrenheit 911*, exposed his exploits. What soldiers had said in the film was edited to make it sound like they had said supported the same perspective as Moore. By the way they said they don't need you to speak for them, so how about you sit back down.

This kind of Pseudo-Political documentaries, are outrageous. It's tainted by the experiences his family had with his father losing his job in his hometown, of Flint, Michigan. So let me understand his logic, the way to fix things, is to support the politicians that want to *obliterate* jobs? I love the flawed logic of people who have dealt with hard times and claim to be victims of the system. Here's a thought. How about taking it out on the lawmakers who set the rules for corporations to follow. Where's the anger that should be aimed their way? Why are they getting off the hook?

There is a very distorted view point, that all businesses are corrupt is a most preposterous notion indeed. Try to convince, these political zealots, such as Moore, Bill Maher, and Arianna Huffington, of this, is like banging your head against a wall. You'll get nowhere fast and end up with one big headache.

One of his most idiotic exploits was his attempt to infiltrate the NRA, to try to bring the organization down. You disagree with a corporation you boycott it, or protest it. You don't try to kill the entity. Now he's just the Neo-Democratic marionette, yes I want to be a real live boy someday. Then cut the strings Pinocchio. If more people took him seriously, than I would consider him a *real* threat. As is I think he's just a mosquito, buzzing around Uncle Sam's head.

Chapter 50 Pop Culture is Beneficial to Society...

… I hope you learned from this, that was my intention. I'm sure that those who are stuck thoroughly in their believes, haven't changed their opinions. For those of you I'm glad. Some might have taken offense. I'm sorry that you did, it wasn't my intention. All I did was take the information that I had and present my opinions about the world we live in. I'm not a propagandist, or a political science major. I'm just doing what I consider my civic duty. Letting people know the truth. The most detrimental tools used to alter our country are, censorship, economic manipulation, half truths, progressivism, corruption, and the most powerful of all, ignorance. You have a powerful tool against them now, knowledge. Thomas Jefferson knew just how important this tool is. That's why he set up his administration as the "People's House," their was no security to the President's lodgings or to the government buildings. Even more he donated his literary collection to be used by the people. Benjamin Franklin pushed the common man to get involved in self improvement, by educating yourself. The Steel Industrial giant Andrew Carnegie, spent his life's fortune building libraries, and other humanitarian efforts. These are only a small few, who saw the potential of this nation and it's people.

Some of you might be wondering about why I didn't comment on some topics. Well, some the issues I don't really consider as detrimental, as the ones discussed. Others I haven't formed an opinion on or come up with a proposed solution to. This is not the end of my career with political writing though, oh no, I'm just getting started. As long as there is corruption in the political organism, and a machine that is supposed to be exposing it, I'll be out there.

An odd effect I've noticed is that Pop Culture has actually produced a cure to the corruption. We have a Pop Culture Revolution in the form of Social and Political satire, with the such programs as *South Park, The Simpsons,* and *House.* On You Tube and other web pages, we have new up coming multi-media that gives us updates on the flaws in our system.

In closing I would like to end with this thought. I think that's fair to make the comparative, of Pop Culture, to that of a disease. Like a disease, this ailment has a treatment. Exorcise the corrosive parts of the structure, and that will allow the rest to regenerate to a robust health. The decaying parts of this structure in this case, are the Hypocrisy and corruption, and for the economy to flourish it must be removed. Then, and only then, can Humanity and Compassion, bloom once more. Then we can experience, for the first time really, True Prosperity.

Thank you, R. C. Seely, the Author

Notes (a place for your comments)...

Notes (a place for your comments)...

_____

_____

_____

_____

_____

_____

_____

_____

_____

_____

_____

_____

_____

_____

_____

_____

Recommended Reading...

The following is a list of books and other reference materials that helped in the writing of this book , to some degree in any case.

Acceptable Risk	By Robin Cook
Alice in Wonderland/ Through the Looking Glass	By Lewis Carol
America's Hidden History	By Kenneth C. Davis
The Art of War	By Sun Tzu
Autobiography of Benjamin Franklin	
The Black Death	By Philip Ziegler
Being George Washington	By Glenn Beck

Bible of Unspeakable Truths	By Greg Gutfield
Broke	By Glenn Beck
Celestine Prophesy	By James Redfield
Conspirata	By Robert Harris
Dante's Inferno	By Dante Alighieri
A Dark History: The Roman Emperors	By Michael Kerrigan
Demian	By Hermann Hesse
Globalization	By Manfred B. Steger
Imperfect Presidents	By Jim Cullen
Marx	By Peter Singer
Meet You in Hell	By Les Standiford
Myth, Lies, and	By John Stossel

Downright Stupidity

Memory's Ghost	By Philip J. Hilts
The Nazi Officer's Wife	By Edith Hahn Beer
Presidential Courage	By Michael R. Beschloss
The Prince	By Niccolo Machiavelli
The Revolution: A Manifesto	By Ron Paul
A Slobbering Love Affair	By Bernie Goldberg
The Secret Service: The Hidden History of an Enigmatic Agency	By Philip H. Melanson
Shadow Party	By David Horowitz and Richard Poe
The Soros Lectures	By George Soros
Vector	By Robin Cook
Vienna 1814	By David King

www.ingramcontent.com/pod-product-compliance
Lightning Source LLC
Chambersburg PA
CBHW081834280526
45789CB00007B/2449